Crafts from Modeling Clay

by Huguette Kirby

Translated by Cheryl L. Smith

Reading Consultant:
Dr. Robert Miller
Professor of Special Education
Minnesota State University, Mankato

Bridgestone Books
an imprint of Capstone Press
Mankato, Minnesota

Table of Contents

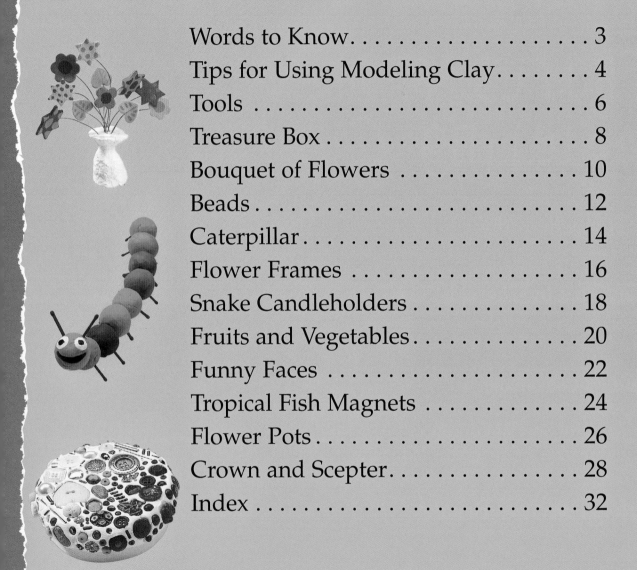

words to know

corrugated cardboard (KOR-uh-gayt-ed KARD-bord)—cardboard formed with
  alternating ridges and grooves on the inside
dowel (DOW-uhl)—a round wooden rod
elastic string (ee-LASS-tik STRING)—thin cord that can stretch out and return to
  its original size and shape
knead (NEED)—to press, fold, and stretch dough or clay to make it smooth
skewer (SKYOO-ur)—a thin stick with a pointed end, usually made from wood
varnish (VAR-nish)—to protect with a thick liquid that dries clear

---

Originally published as *Pâtes á Modeler,* © 1998 Editions Milan.

Bridgestone Books are published by Capstone Press
151 Good Counsel Drive, P.O. Box 669, Mankato, Minnesota 56002
http://www.capstone-press.com

For infor~~mation~~ ~~ss,~~
151 Good Cou~~nsel~~ ~~ta 56002~~

Library of Congress Cataloging-in-Publication Data
Kirby, Huguette.
  [Pâtes á modeler. English]
  Crafts from modeling clay/by Huguette Kirby; translated by
Cheryl L. Smith.
    p. cm.—(Step by step)
    Translation of: Pâtes á modeler.
    Includes index.
    Summary: Provides instructions for creating such simple objects
as a treasure box, beads, snake candleholders, and a flower frame.
    ISBN 0-7368-1477-9 (hardcover)
    1. Clay—Juvenile literature. 2. Handicraft—Juvenile literature.
[1. Clay. 2. Handicraft.] I. Title. II. Step by step (Mankato, Minn.)
TT916 .K57 2003
731.4'2—dc21
                                                2002002175

1 2 3 4 5 6 07 06 05 04 03 02

Editor:
Rebecca Glaser

Photographs:
Milan/Dominique Chauvet;
Capstone Press/Gary Sundermeyer

Graphic Design:
Sarbacane

Design Production:
Steve Christensen

Tips for Using Modeling Clay

You can use modeling clay to create funny faces, large beads, snake candleholders, flowering frames, and many other objects. Make sure you use the right type of clay for each activity.

Air-Dry Clay

This type of clay is gray or brown-orange. After drying, it can be sanded, painted, or varnished.

Colored Modeling Clay

This colored clay does not dry out. It can be used again and the colors do not mix.

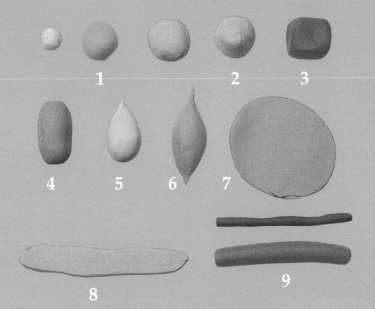

Super Light clay

This white clay is five times lighter than other clays. It dries in the air. After drying, it can be polished, cut, pierced, glued, painted, or varnished.

Basic Shapes

1. Round balls
2. Flattened balls
3. Cubes
4. Lengthened balls
5. Lengthened balls pinched on one end
6. Lengthened balls pinched on both ends
7. Pancakes
8. Strips
9. Sausages

Tools

rolling pin

bowl

paint

butter knife

paintbrush

spoon

wooden skewer

tacky glue

cookie cutters

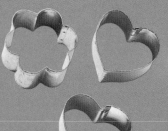

6

Use With Adult Help:

utility knife

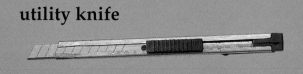

embroidery needle

friendly advice

- Before working with clay, cover the table with a plastic sheet or garbage bag to avoid getting the table dirty.
- Wash your hands well before and after using the clay.
- For better results, knead the clay before making a project. If the clay is cold and hard, it will warm in your hands and become softer.
- When you use clays of different colors, wash your hands between each color.
- Modeling clay rolls out easily with a rolling pin. Put a little cooking oil on the rolling pin with your fingers so that the clay does not stick.
- For air-dry clay and super light clay, wet your fingers once in a while to keep the clay from drying out while you are working.
- To connect two pieces of clay, wet them with your fingers.
- Store your unused clay in a plastic container.

Treasure Box

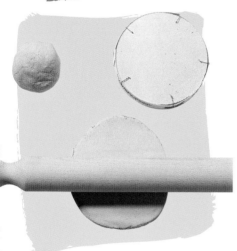

1 Make a ball of clay the size of an orange. Roll it out with a rolling pin to form a pancake. Spread the top of the clay with glue and place the box cover on top of it.

2 Fold the clay over the edges of the cover. With the butter knife, cut off the extra clay.

3 Cover the surface of the clay with glue. Press buttons, beads, shells, or stones into it.

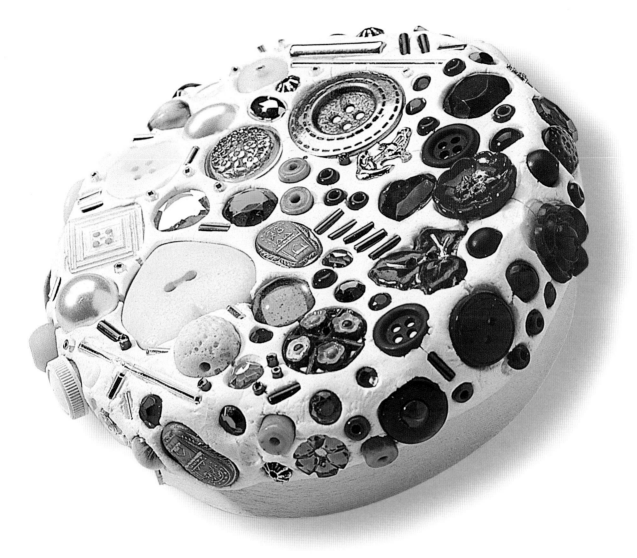

Start a collection of rocks, buttons, shells, or stickers. Keep your collection in your box so you do not lose it.

Bouquet of Flowers

You Will Need:
- **Super light clay**
- **Rolling pin**
- **Cookie cutters**
- **Wire**
- **Paint**
- **Paintbrush**

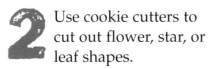

2 Use cookie cutters to cut out flower, star, or leaf shapes.

1 Make a ball of clay the size of a golf ball. Then roll it out with the rolling pin.

3 Poke wire through the shapes to make stems. Let the shapes dry for 24 hours. Then paint them.

4 With more clay, make a ball the size of an orange. Shape it into a vase. Flatten the top and the bottom.

You also can make a bouquet of people. Glue photos of your friends or family on the heads of people you create.

5 Stick your flowers, leaves, and stars into the vase.

11

Beads

You Will Need:
- **Super light clay**
- **Wooden skewer**
- **Paint**
- **Paintbrush**
- **Elastic string**

2 Paint your beads with bright colors. When the beads are dry, paint all sizes of dots on them.

1 Form little balls of clay in your hands. Pierce them with a wooden skewer and let them dry for 12 hours.

3 String the beads on elastic string to make necklaces or bracelets.

12

To make cube-shaped beads, make small balls and squeeze them a little between your fingers.

13

caterpillar

3 Paint eyes and a mouth on one ball. Poke toothpicks into the balls to create legs and antennas. Paint the toothpicks. Twist the balls so the legs face down.

1 Form clay balls and paint them before they dry.

2 Ask an adult to poke holes through the balls with a large embroidery needle and string them on elastic string. Add a little clay to the balls on each end to patch the needle holes.

14

A caterpillar breathes through nine pairs of small openings called spiracles (**SPEER**-uh-kuhlss). One pair is on each body section.

15

Flower Frames

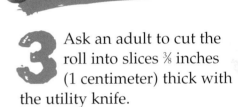

You Will Need:
- **Colored modeling clay**
- **Utility knife**
- **Corrugated cardboard**
- **Tacky glue**

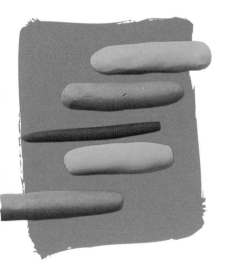

1 Form four fat sausages of clay and one skinny one.

2 Put them all together with the skinny one in the middle. Press them lightly together until they stick together and form a larger roll.

3 Ask an adult to cut the roll into slices ⅜ inches (1 centimeter) thick with the utility knife.

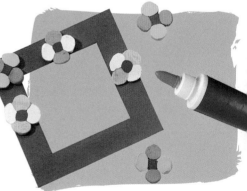

4 Ask an adult to cut out a frame from the cardboard. Paint the cardboard and glue the flowers onto the frame.

16

6 To make your frame stand up, cut a 2-inch (5-centimeter) strip of cardboard. Fold it into a triangle and glue it to the back of your frame.

5 Glue a photo on a piece of cardboard the same size as your frame. Glue this piece of cardboard to the back of the frame.

Snake candleholders

Be Careful! An adult must light the candle.

1 Make a long clay sausage and roll it around a candle without squeezing the clay too much. Let the head and the tail stick out a little bit. Bend a piece of wire in half and stick it into the mouth.

2 Let the snake dry for two days. Then remove the candle. Paint the snake one color and let it dry.

3 Paint eyes on the snake. Then paint a design on the snake.

18

Snakes flick their tongues in and out to smell. Snakes' tongues pick up scents. Snakes bring their tongues inside their mouths so the scents touch their Jacobson's organ. This mouth part senses smell.

Fruits and Vegetables

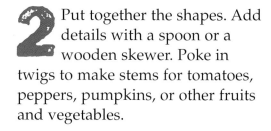

2 Put together the shapes. Add details with a spoon or a wooden skewer. Poke in twigs to make stems for tomatoes, peppers, pumpkins, or other fruits and vegetables.

1 Make round, long, or flat shapes that look like vegetables and fruits.

The white parts of a cauliflower that you eat actually are flower buds. Most of the cauliflower grown in the Unites States comes from California.

Funny Faces

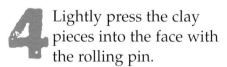

3 On the face, add little balls, strings, or strips of clay to create the eyes, mouth, nose, and cheeks.

2 Slightly roll out the clay with a rolling pin.

4 Lightly press the clay pieces into the face with the rolling pin.

1 Make an oval-shaped ball for the face and six or seven small balls for the hair.

5 Paint a piece of cardboard. Glue your funny face to the piece of cardboard. Then ask an adult to cut out a frame the same size as the piece of cardboard. Glue the frame to the cardboard.

23

Tropical Fish Magnets

You Will Need:
- Colored modeling clay
- Tacky glue
- Magnets
- Spoon
- Wooden skewer

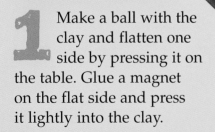

1 Make a ball with the clay and flatten one side by pressing it on the table. Glue a magnet on the flat side and press it lightly into the clay.

2 Create the shape of a fish. Decorate it with a spoon, a wooden skewer, or small bits of clay.

A tropical lionfish has 18 sharp, pointed spines that produce a poison. The poison can kill other animals.

25

Flower Pots

You Will Need:
- **Air-dry clay**
- **Clay flower pot**
- **Butter knife**
- **Wooden skewer**

1 Cover a small flower pot with clay and form a lip around the top.

2 Create eyes, nose, cheeks, chin, and ears.

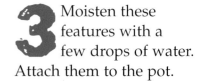

3 Moisten these features with a few drops of water. Attach them to the pot.

4 With a butter knife, trace a line for the mouth. Then poke a hole in the middle of the eyes with a wooden skewer. Let your pot dry for two days.

26

After your pot is dry, choose a plant that will look like hair. Put plenty of fresh soil in the pot and place the plant in it. Put your plant in a sunny place and remember to water it.

27

Crown and Scepter

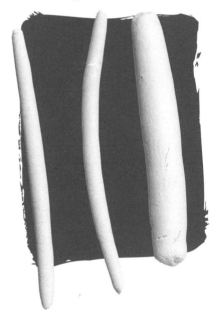

1 Make two small clay sausages and one large one, all about 18 inches (46 centimeters) long.

2 Flatten out the large sausage with a rolling pin.

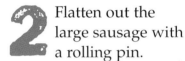

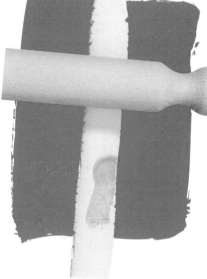

3 Dip your fingers in water and moisten the clay. Place the small sausages on the flattened one. Form the base of the crown by attaching the two ends.

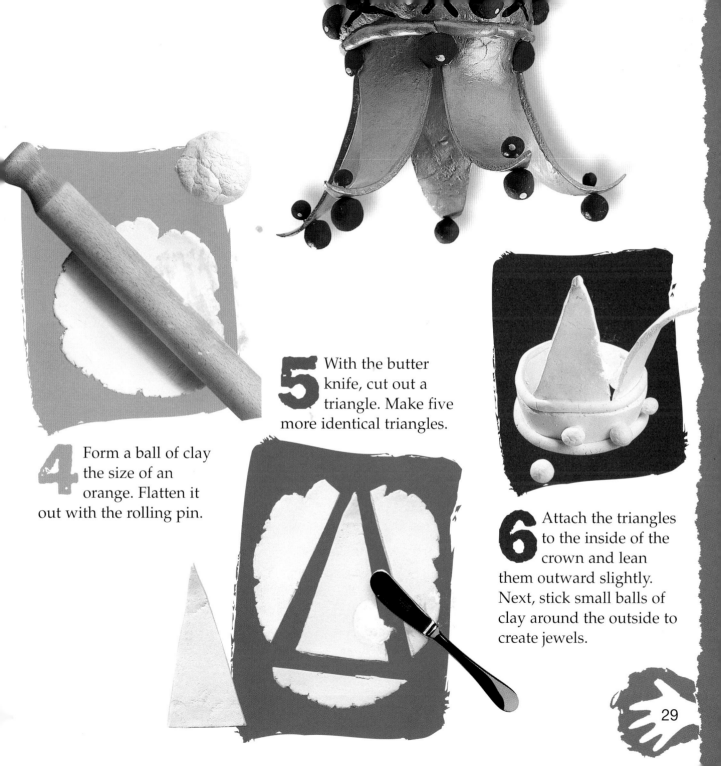

5 With the butter knife, cut out a triangle. Make five more identical triangles.

4 Form a ball of clay the size of an orange. Flatten it out with the rolling pin.

6 Attach the triangles to the inside of the crown and lean them outward slightly. Next, stick small balls of clay around the outside to create jewels.

29

→ **Kings and queens sometimes carry a scepter. This jeweled rod is a symbol of power.**

7 Make more small balls and attach them to the points of the crown with toothpicks. Paint the crown with gold paint and the jewels with other colors.

8 To make a scepter to go with your crown, form a ball and push it onto the dowel. Add small, crownlike shapes. Paint the scepter to match the crown.

index